AKASHIC DREAMING

A Selection of
Inspiring Drawings
for the Heart
and Soul

Designs by **Tanith Hare**
Edited by **Zak Buchanan**

First published by Ultimate World Publishing 2024
Copyright © 2024 Tanith Hare

ISBN

Paperback: 978-1-923255-09-8
Ebook: 978-1-923255-10-4

Designed by Tanith, digitally edited by Zak and Nik. No AI has been used in my creations.

Cover design: Ultimate World Publishing
Layout and typesetting: Ultimate World Publishing
Editor: Alex Floyd-Douglass

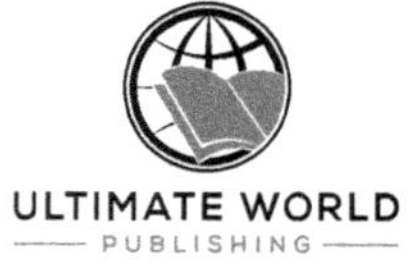

Ultimate World Publishing
Diamond Creek,
Victoria Australia 3089
www.writeabook.com.au

Contents

"Life is but a dream, within a dream."

(Edgar Allan Poe)

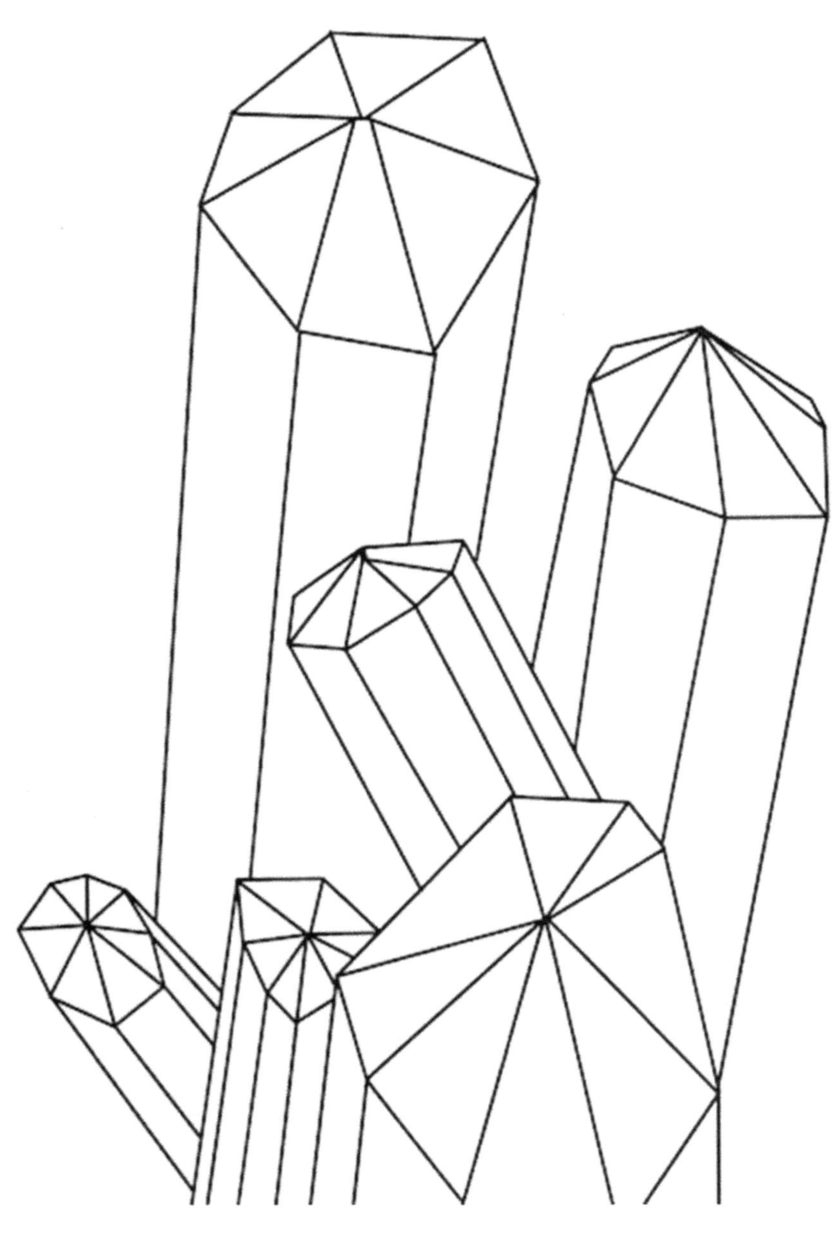

For My Daughter, Juliette

"Young people are a great inspiration and keep me young at heart."
(Tanith Hare)

Known to have created her whole life, Tanith has expressed herself through art and craft, creating many different pieces in various mediums and textiles, including anything from drawing and painting to collage, sewing, and sculpture.

After studying fashion and bringing her only child into the world, Tanith went into dressmaking – alongside other mediums such as candlemaking, wood and metal work, and wool crafts such as spinning yarn, felting, and weaving.

Now in her 40s, Tanith has collected all of her drawings and sketches over the years –including both recent and remastered sketches – to curate a final body of work for the pages of this expressive colouring book for you to enjoy.

Akashic Dreaming is a momentum of expression inspired by Tanith's daughter, Juliette, who has blessed her daily with her kind heart, passion for life, and generosity. As a young adult, colouring is one of Juliette's creative pursuits, and she regularly expresses the needs of the youth when they converse and relays their struggles today.

Having travelled the world and visited several countries, Tanith has drawn in remembrance of the famous sites and scenery of the vast lands—places held dear, moments, memories, and still life—the mysterious and enchanting places of the world and the places that create hope and instil peace within.

As a nature lover inspired to draw memories – along with inspitation from Juliette – Tanith has included many abstract mandalas, flowers, and plants throughout the book.

First published in the '90s, Tanith has devoted her time to raising her daughter and welfare practices, such as behavioural studies, after studying psychology at university. On reflection, Tanith says, *"Art therapy is a positive outlet for bottled-up emotions that uses skills to assist with open-minded youth."*

Tanith remembers her younger years and all the joys, pains, and torments of becoming an adult. This book is intended for its artists to use their emotions and embrace the feeling of moving forward in life through self-development and growth.

"With an ever-changing world, using your creativity can ease the process."
(Tanith Hare)

Tanith wishes to thank her daughter and today's youth for her growth. She would also like to thank those she's met and developed rapport with throughout her professional career.

As we develop and grow continuously throughout life, her wish is for you to enjoy the expression of creativity and mental release in this book through joy, truth, and beauty as you colour to express feelings, emotions, and thoughts.

Use this book as inspiration and a way to open your mind to the possibilities of colouring and being creative. You might just surprise yourself.

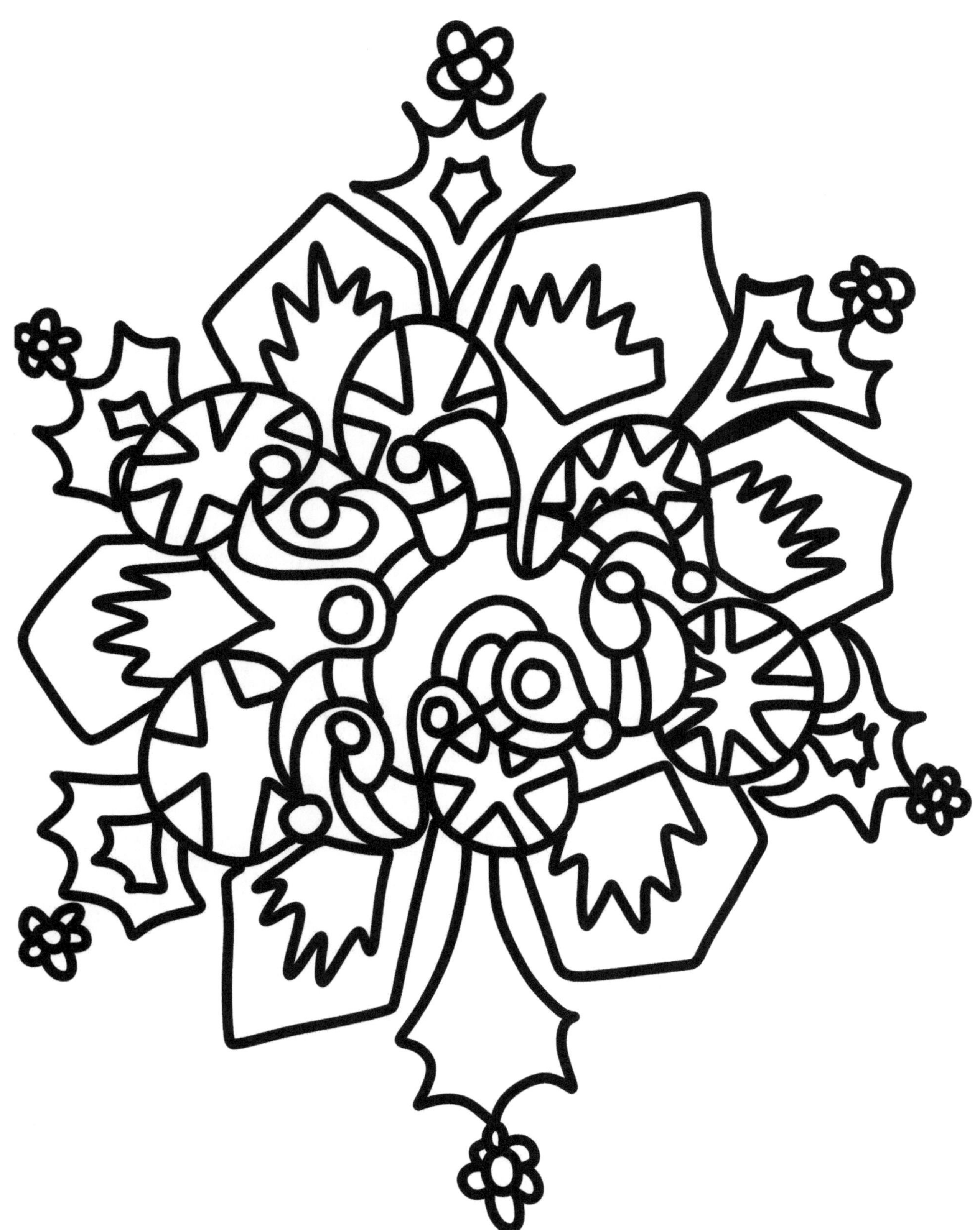

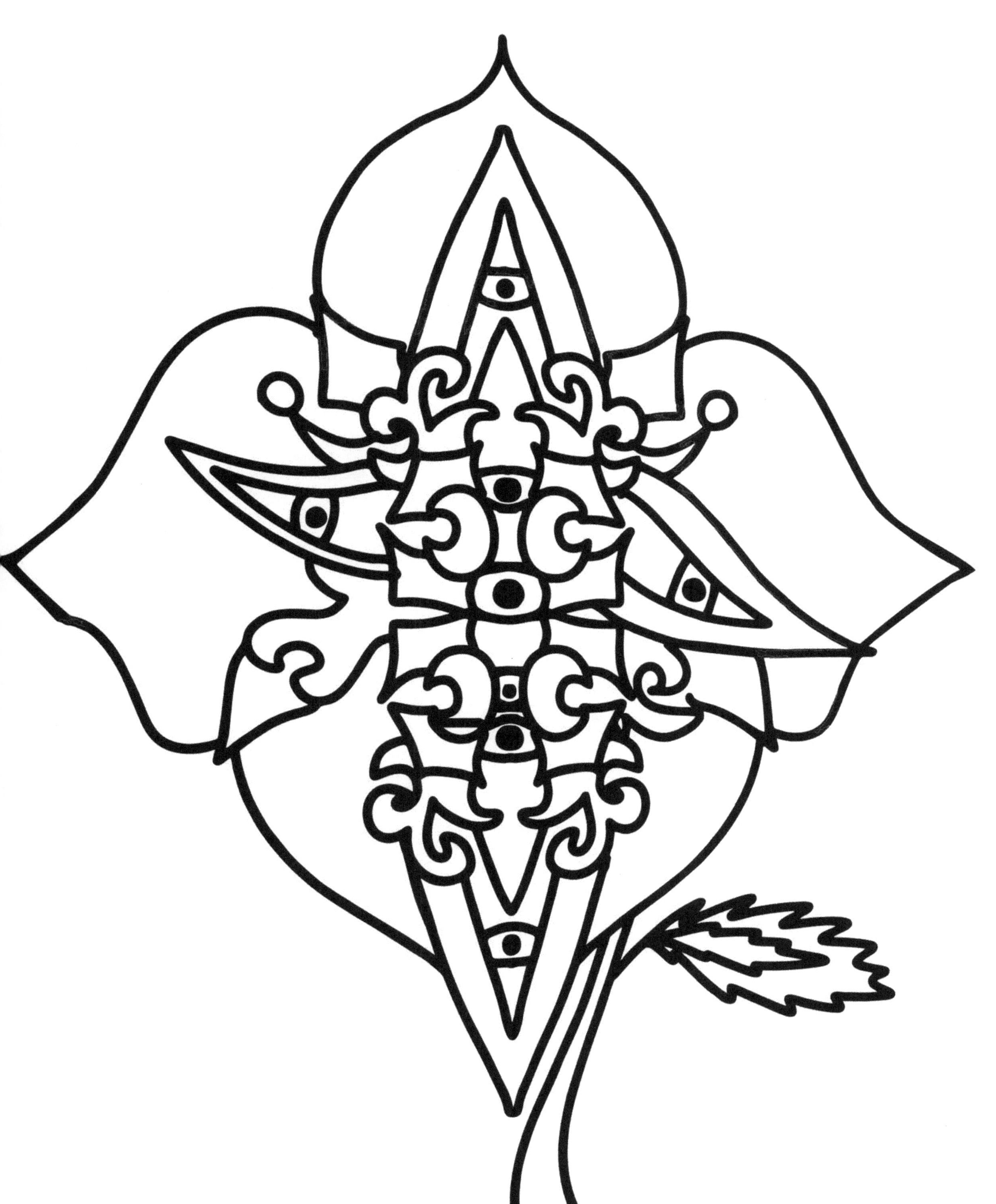

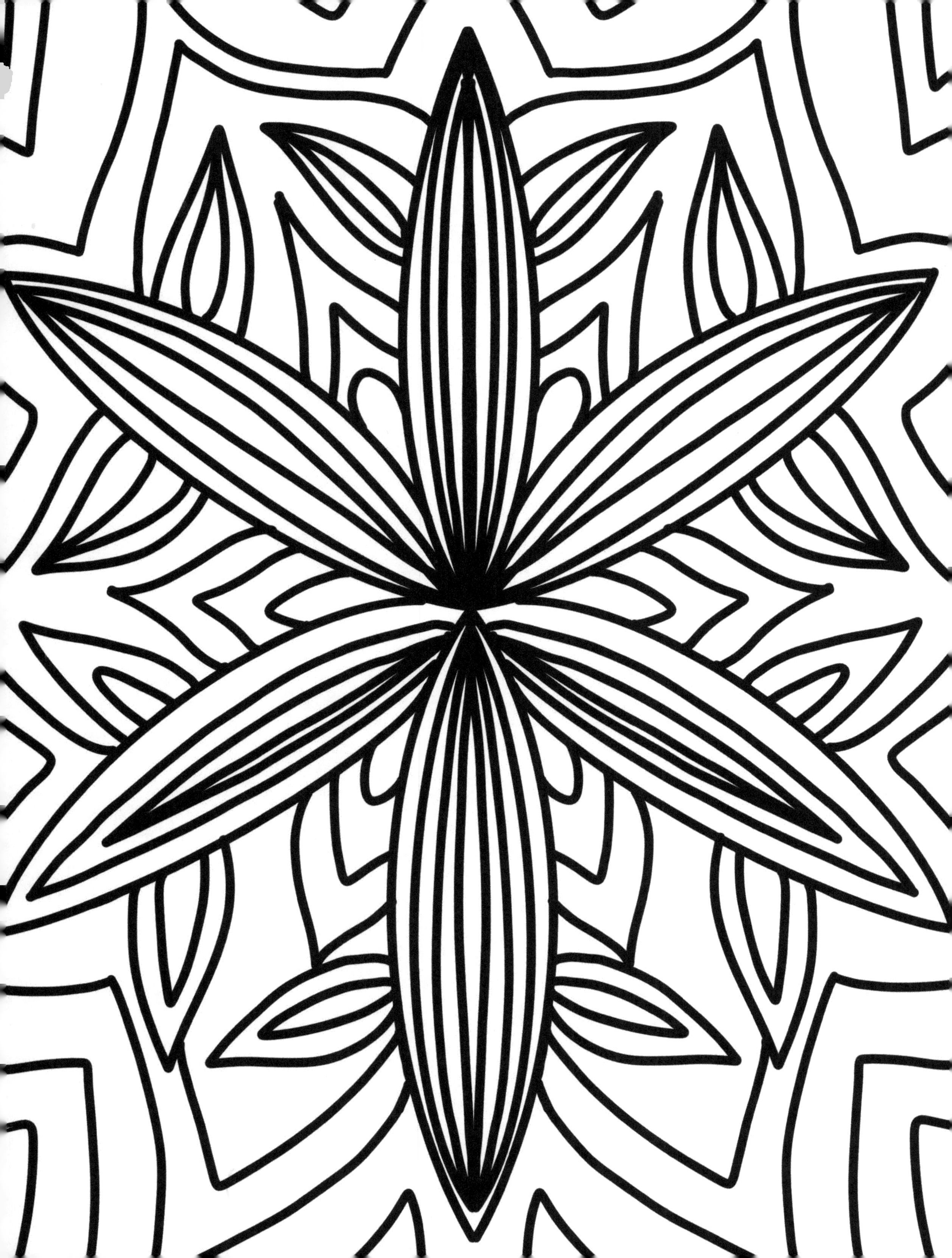

"Our own life has to be our message."
(Thich Nhat Hanh)

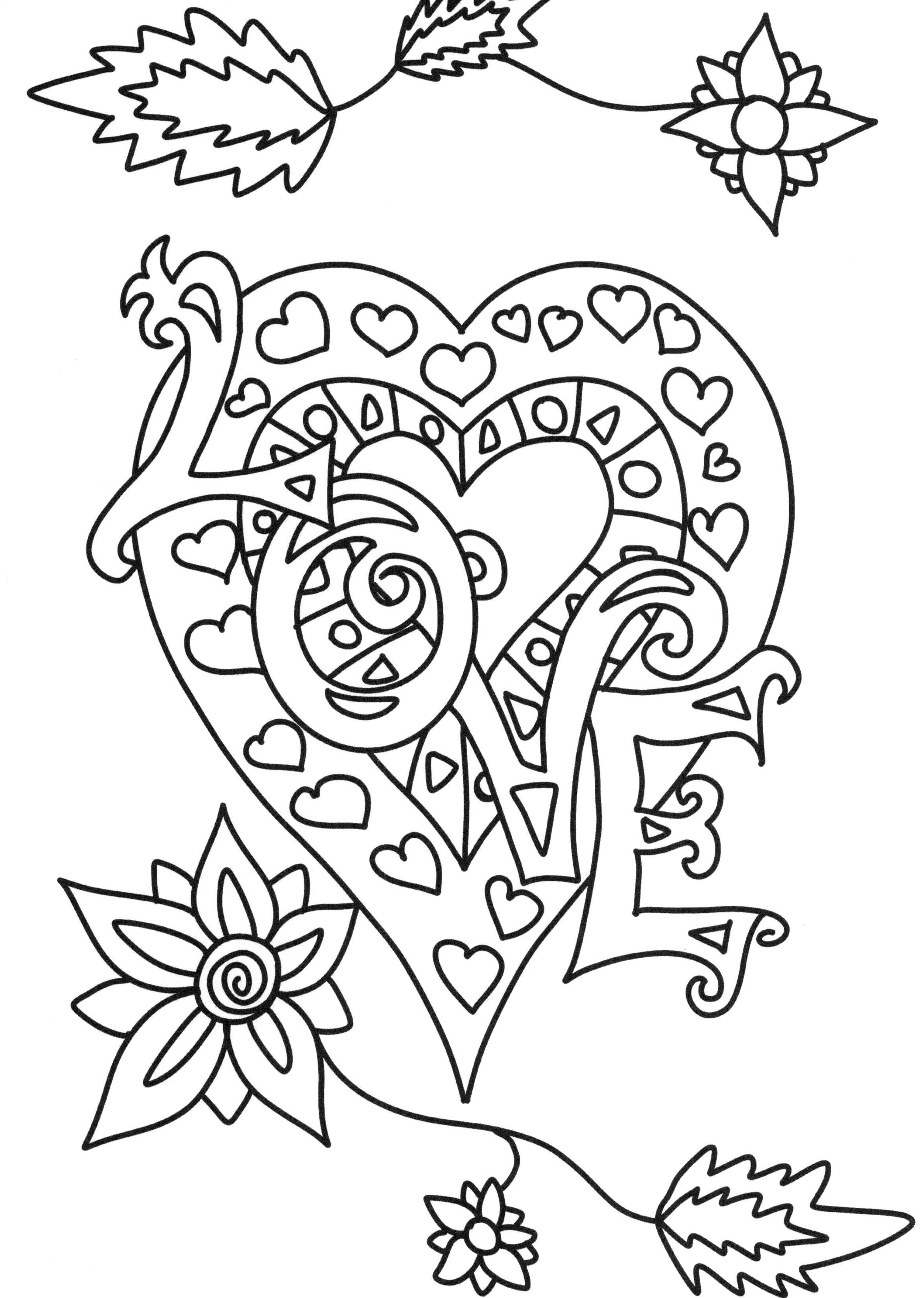

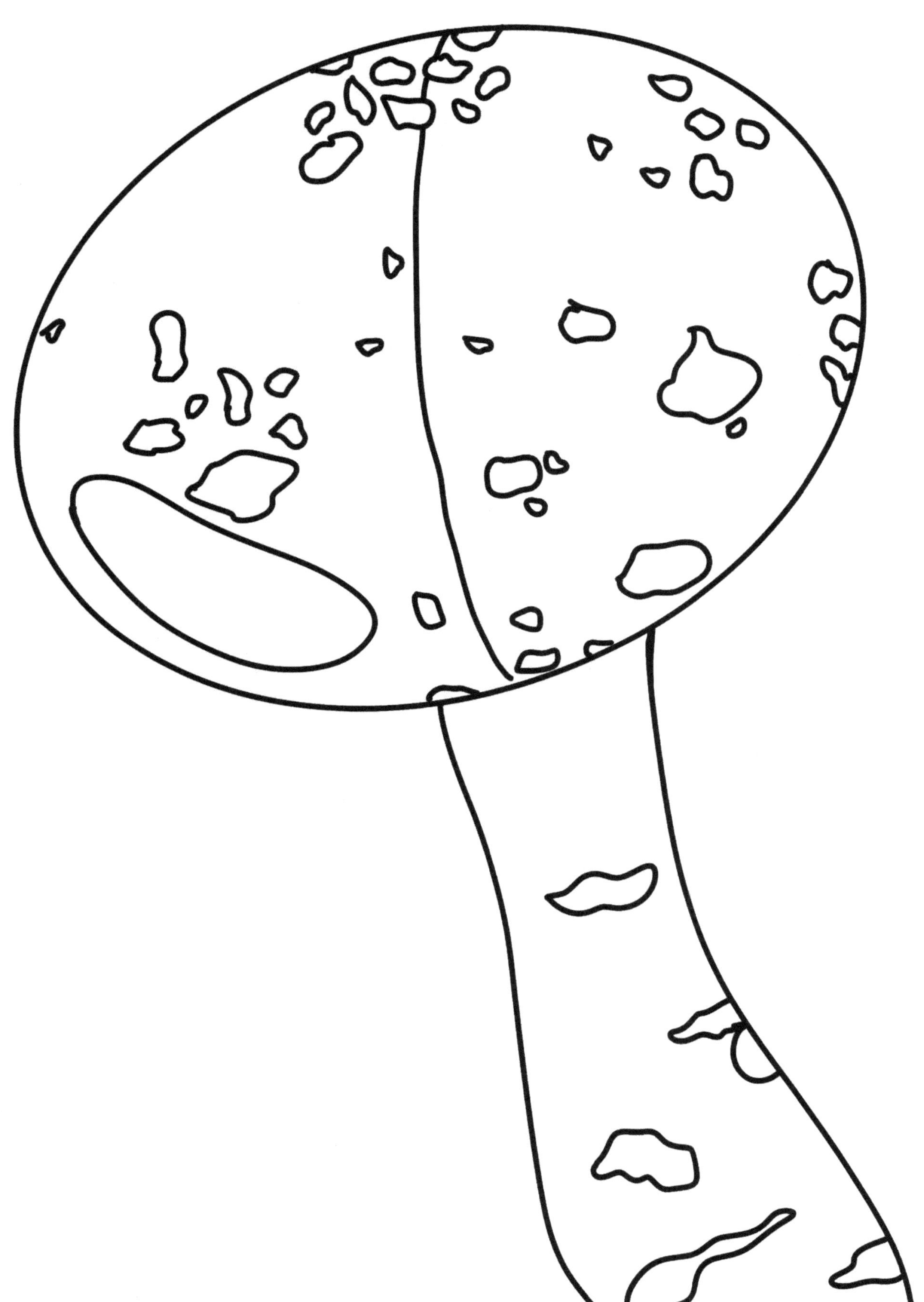

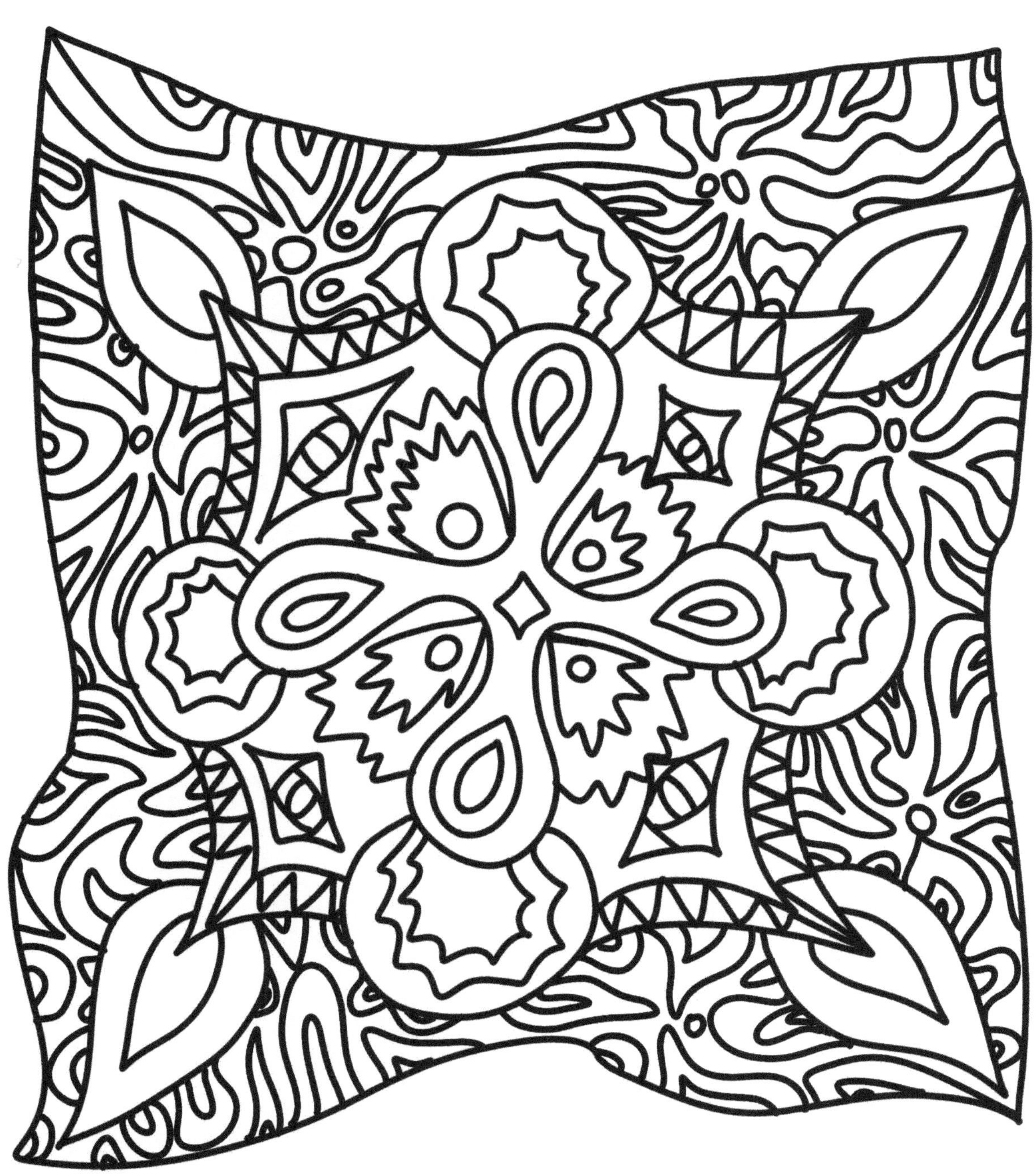

"We will be more successful in all our endeavours if we can
let go of the habit of running all the time, and take little pauses to
relax and re-center ourselves. And we'll also have a lot more joy in living."
(Thich Nhat Hanh)

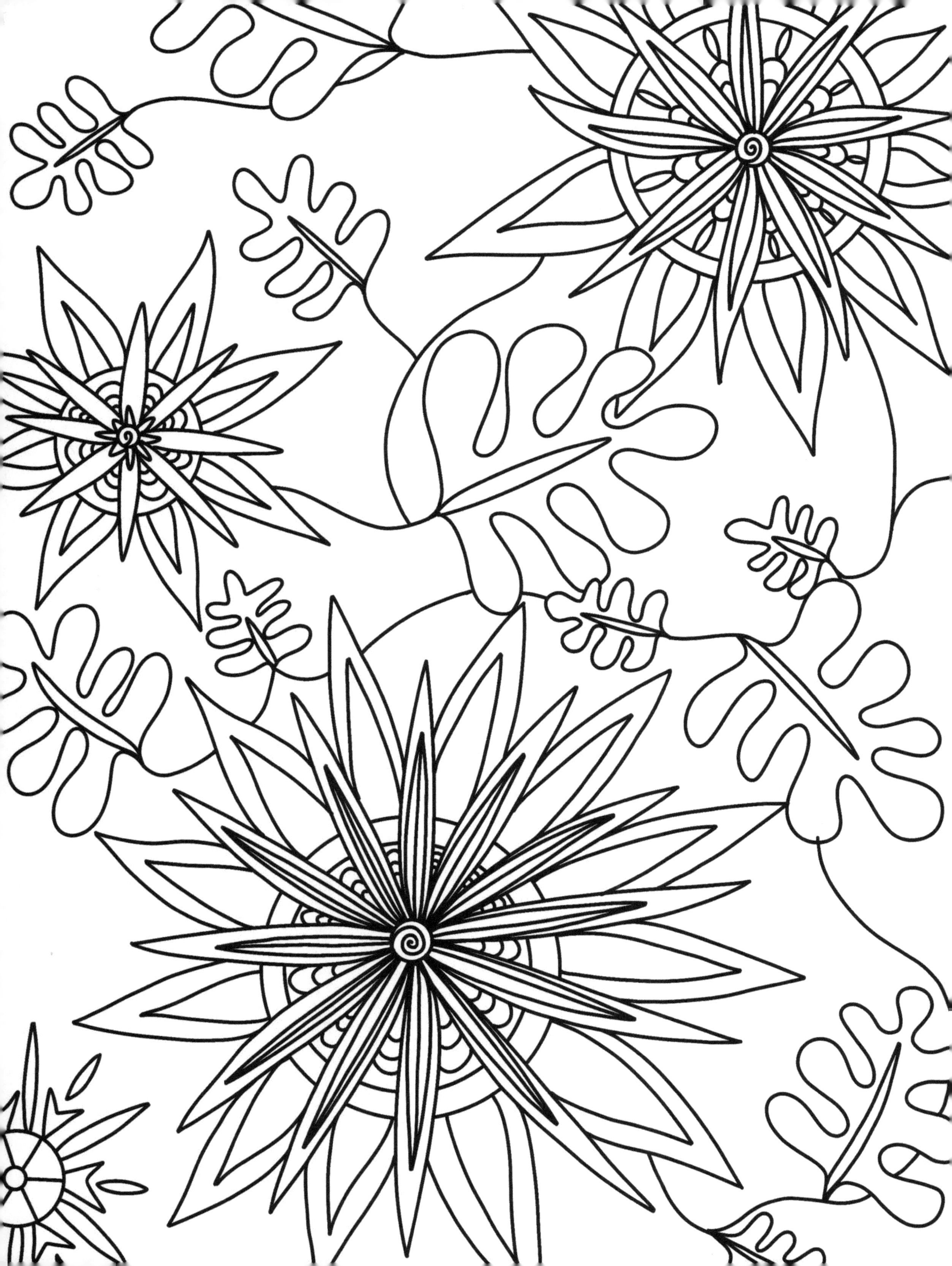

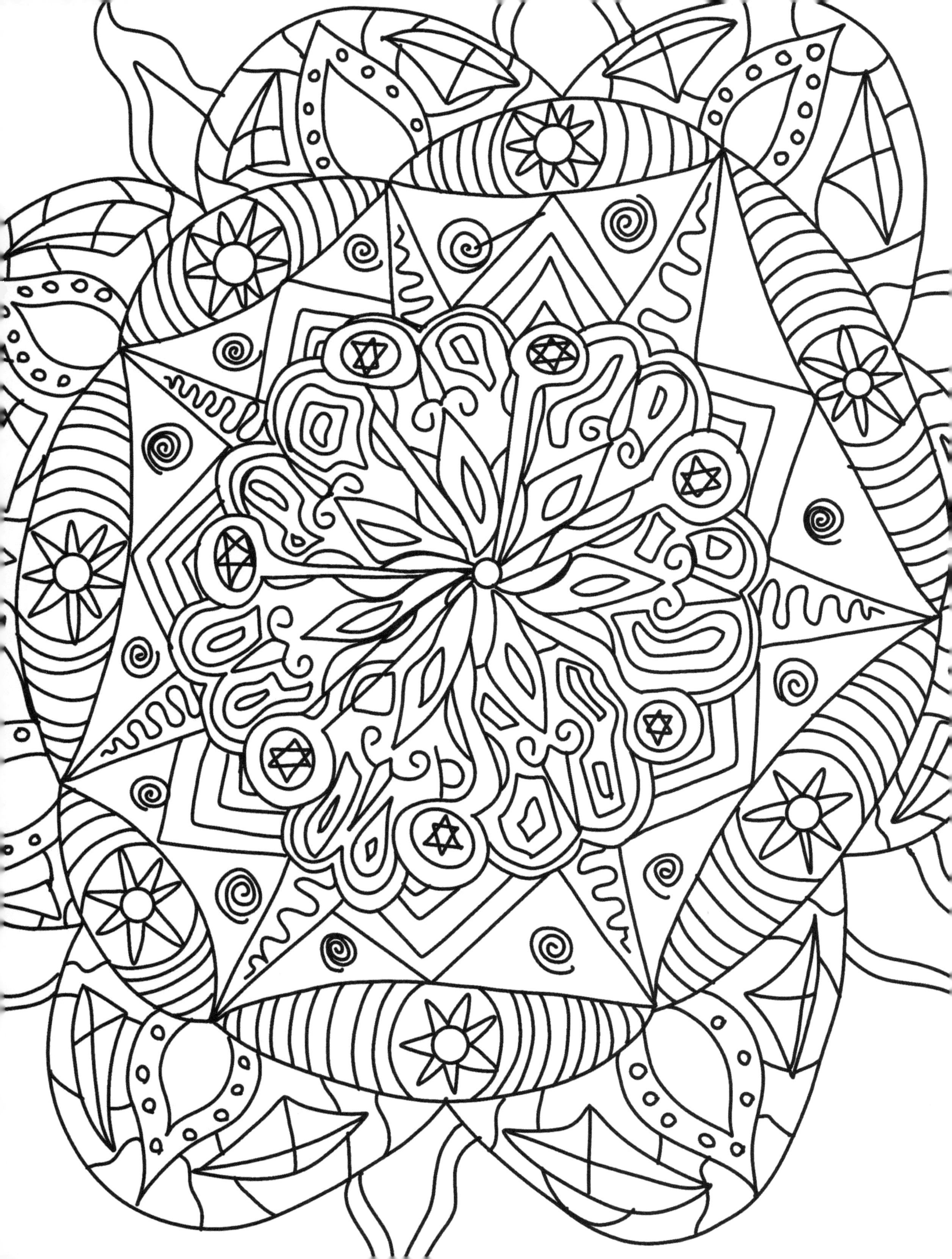

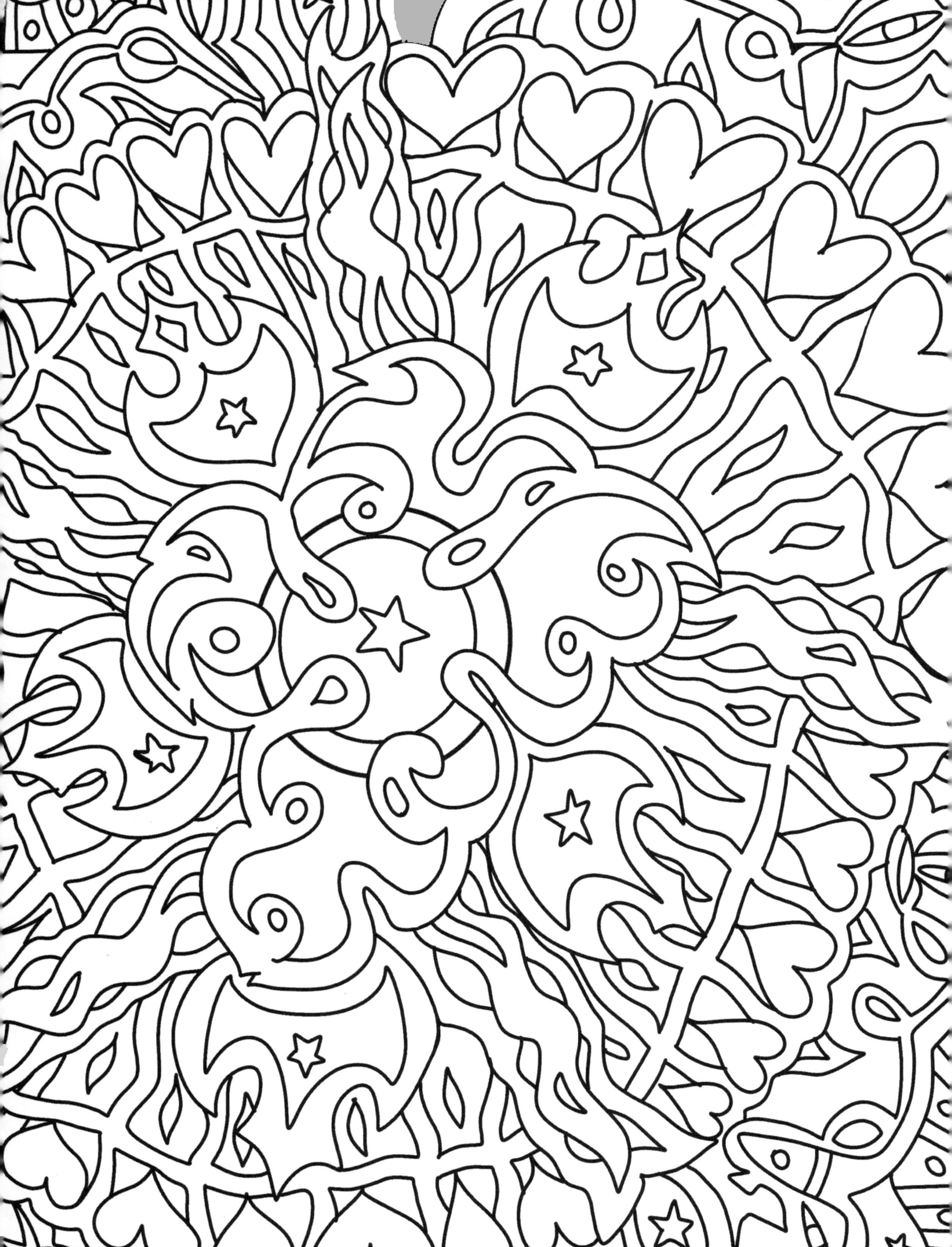

"I was never really insane except upon occasions when my heart was touched."
(Edgar Allan Poe)

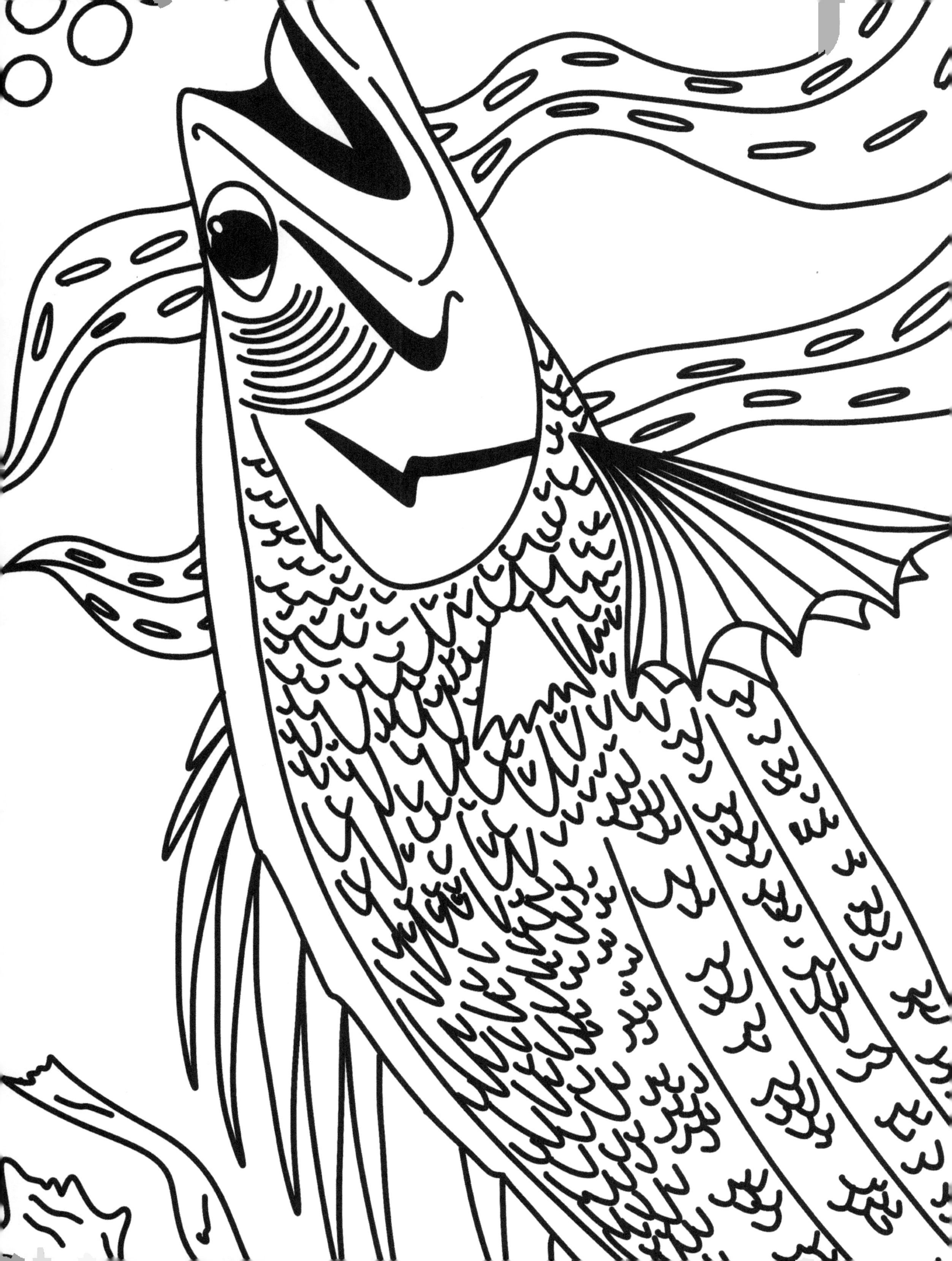

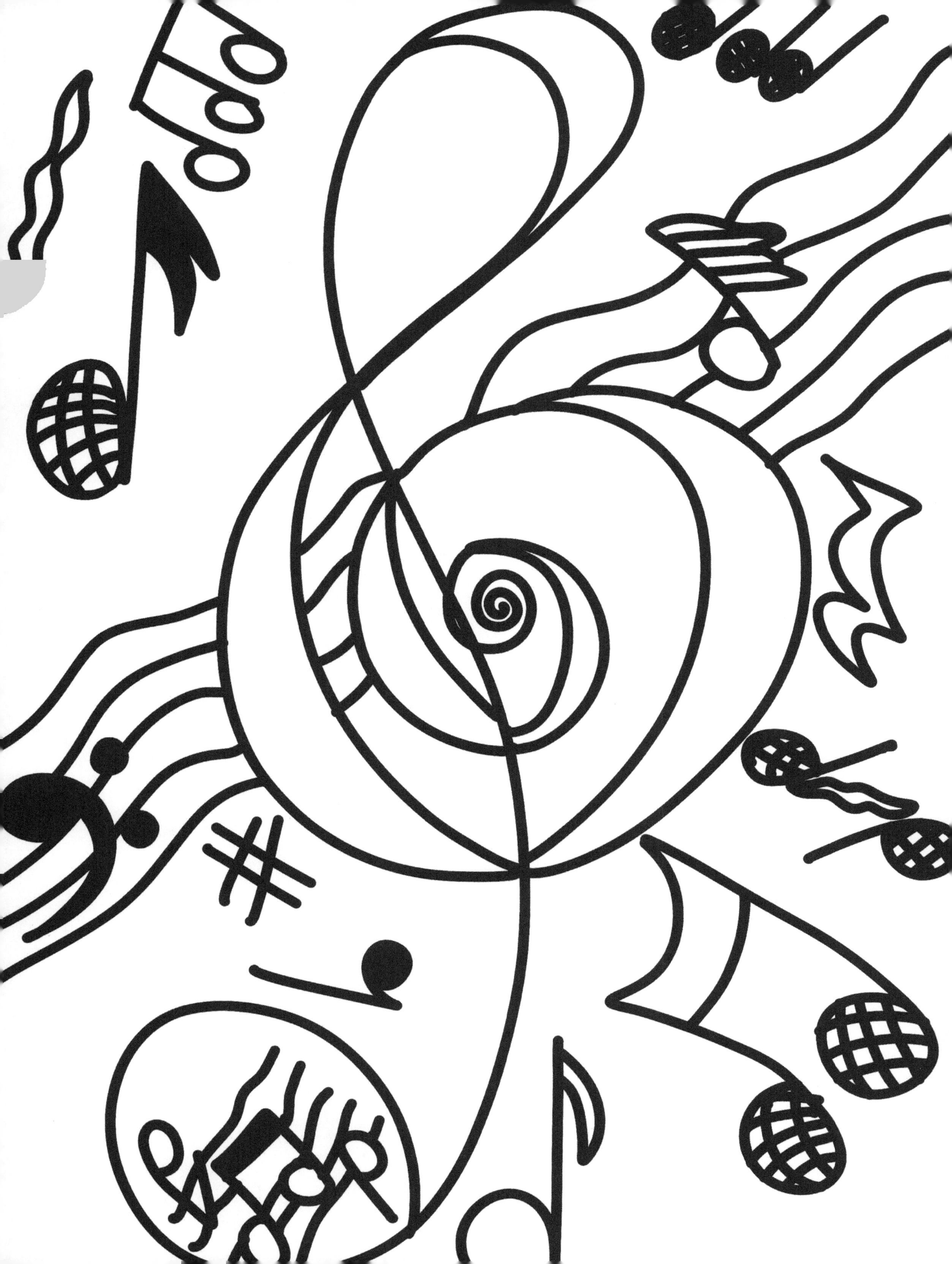

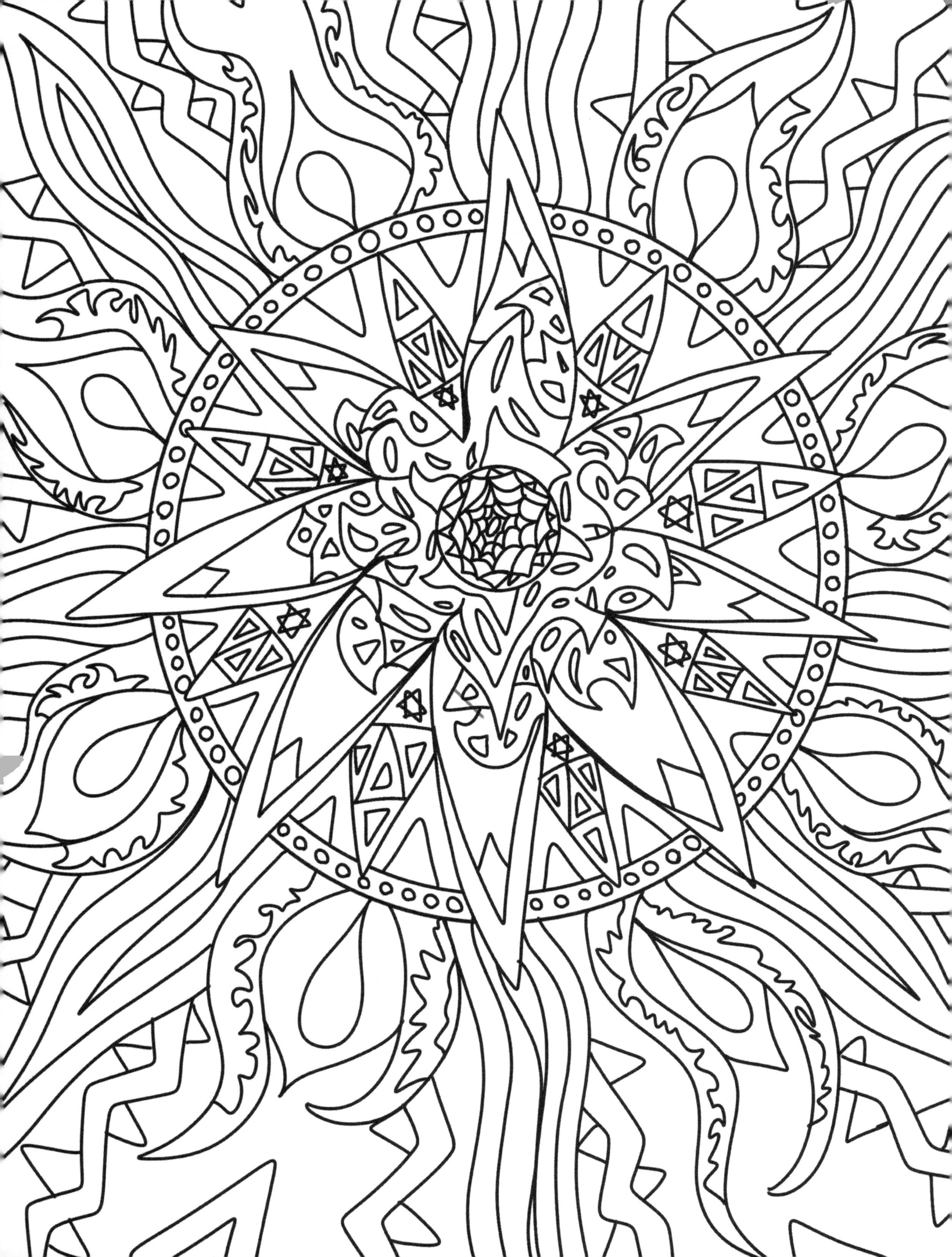

*"Do not judge me by my success, judge me by
how many times I fell down and got back up again."*
(Nelson Mandela)

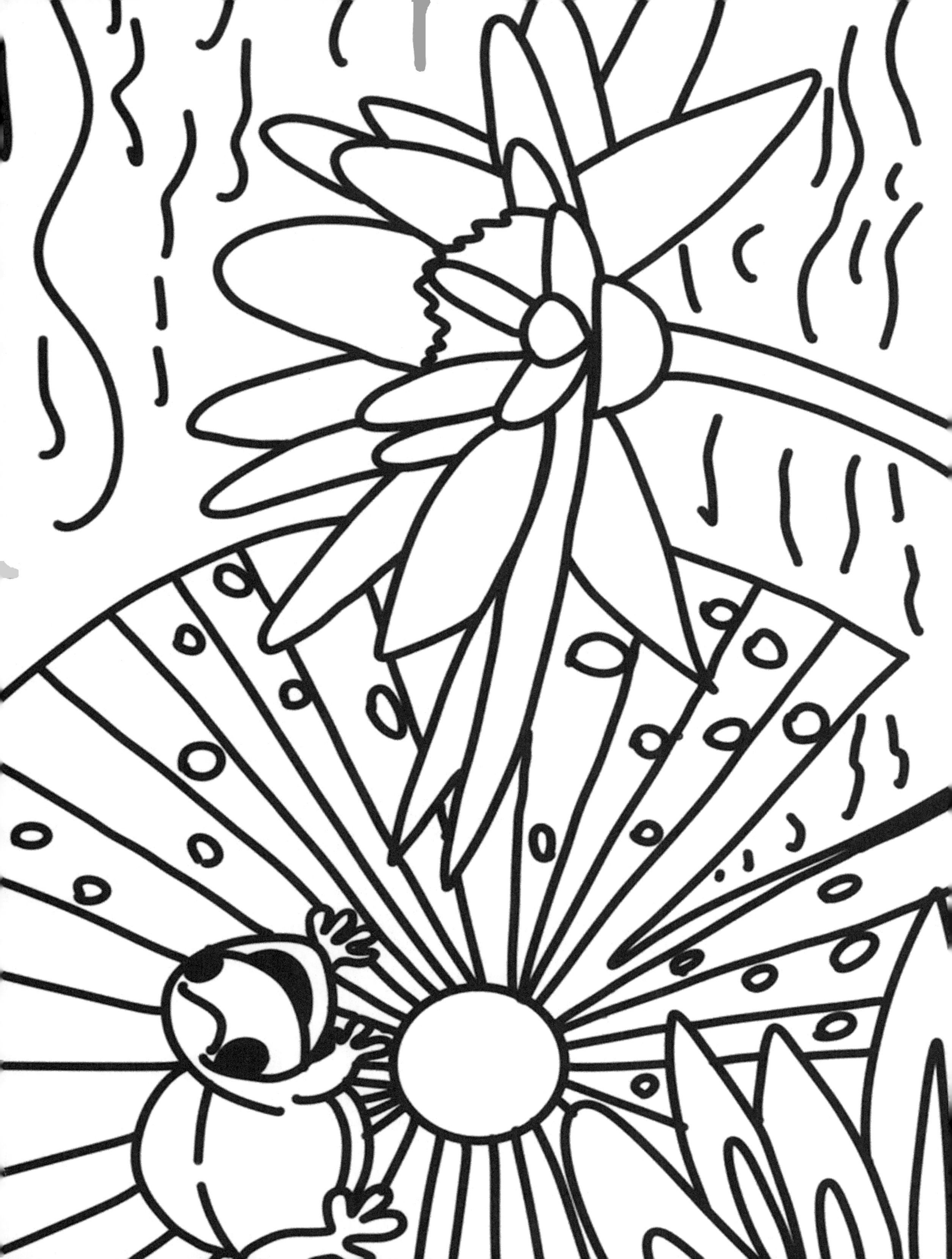

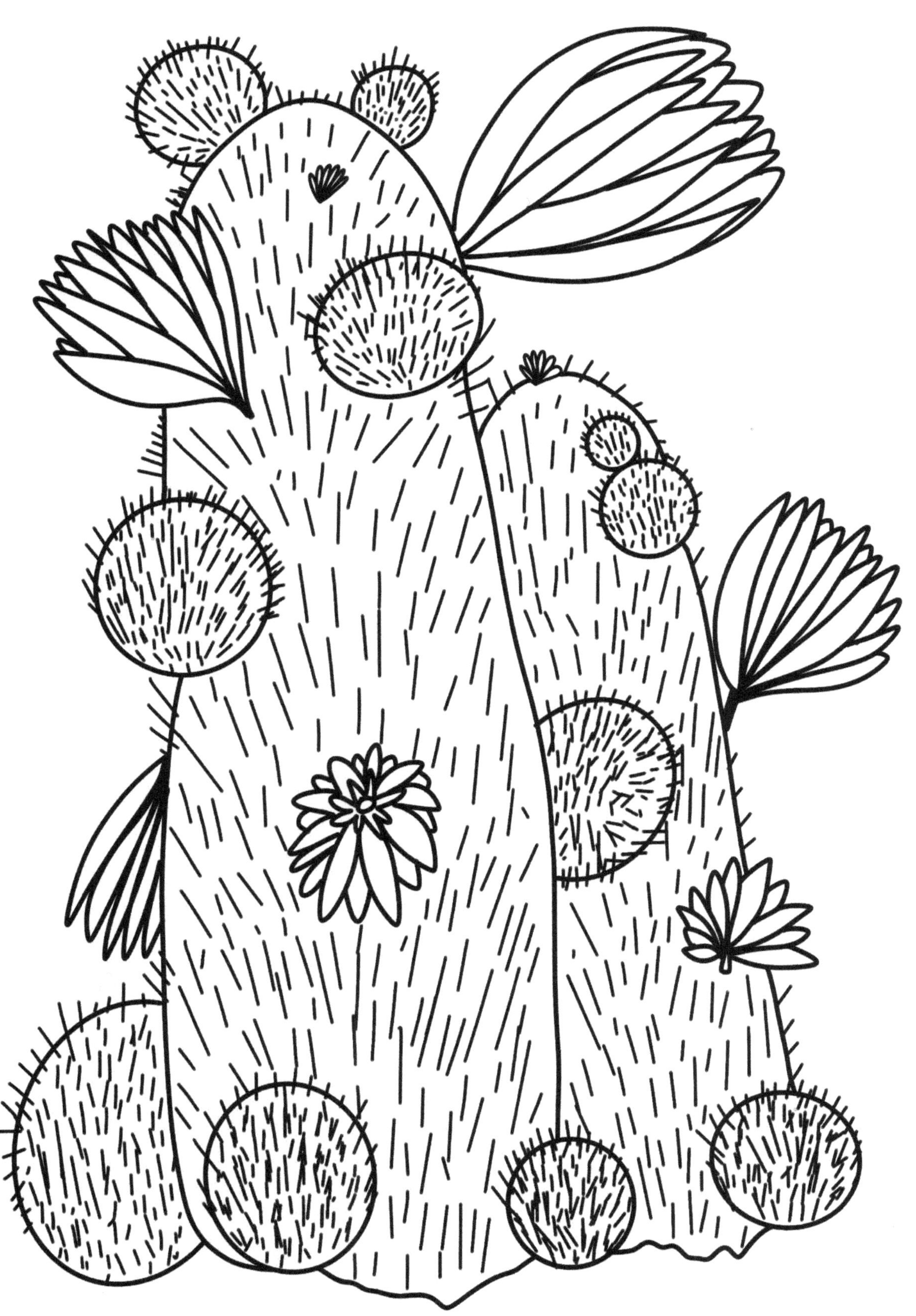

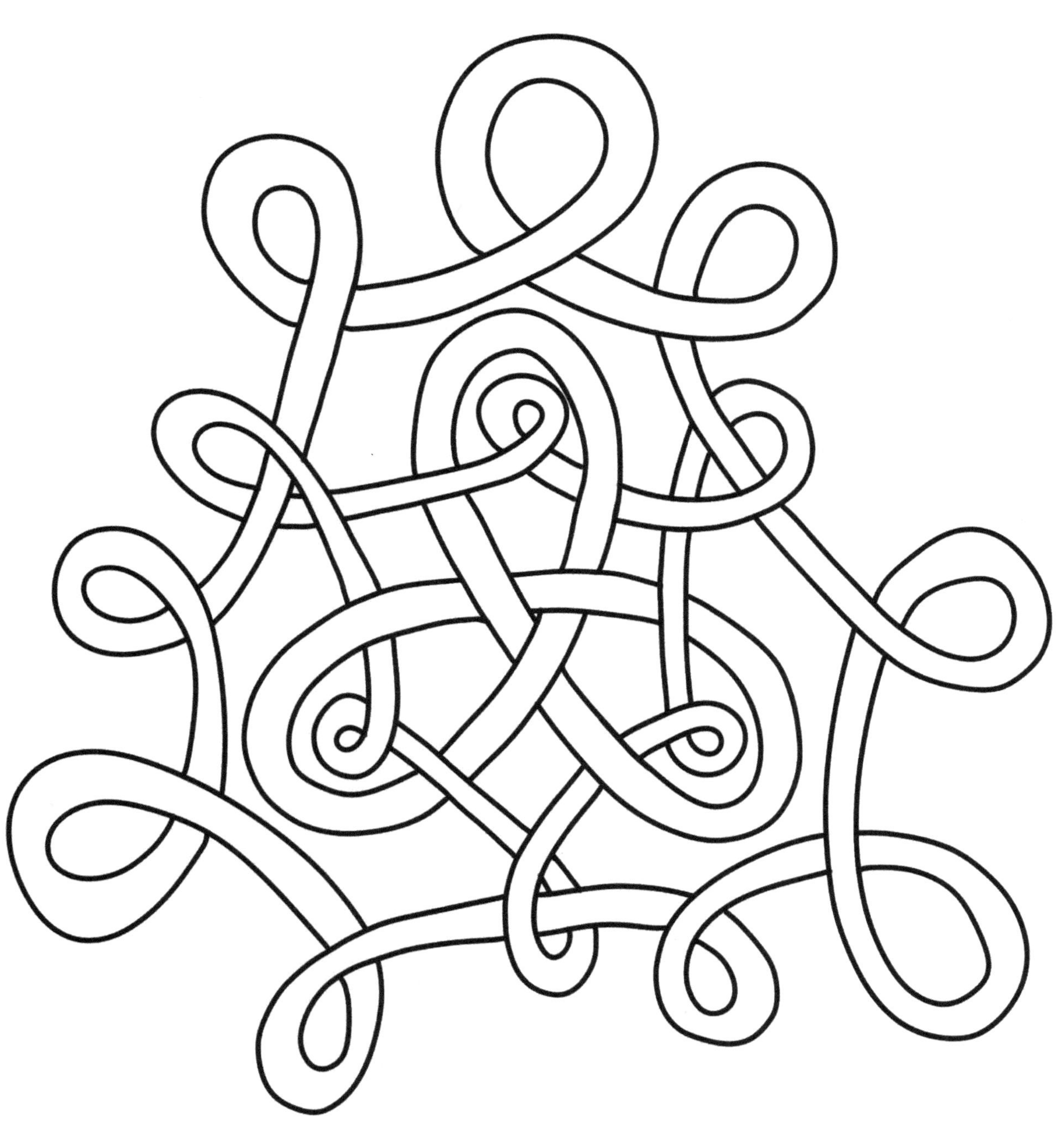

*"Courage isn't having the strength to go on,
it is going on when you don't have the strength."*
(Napoleon Bonaparte)

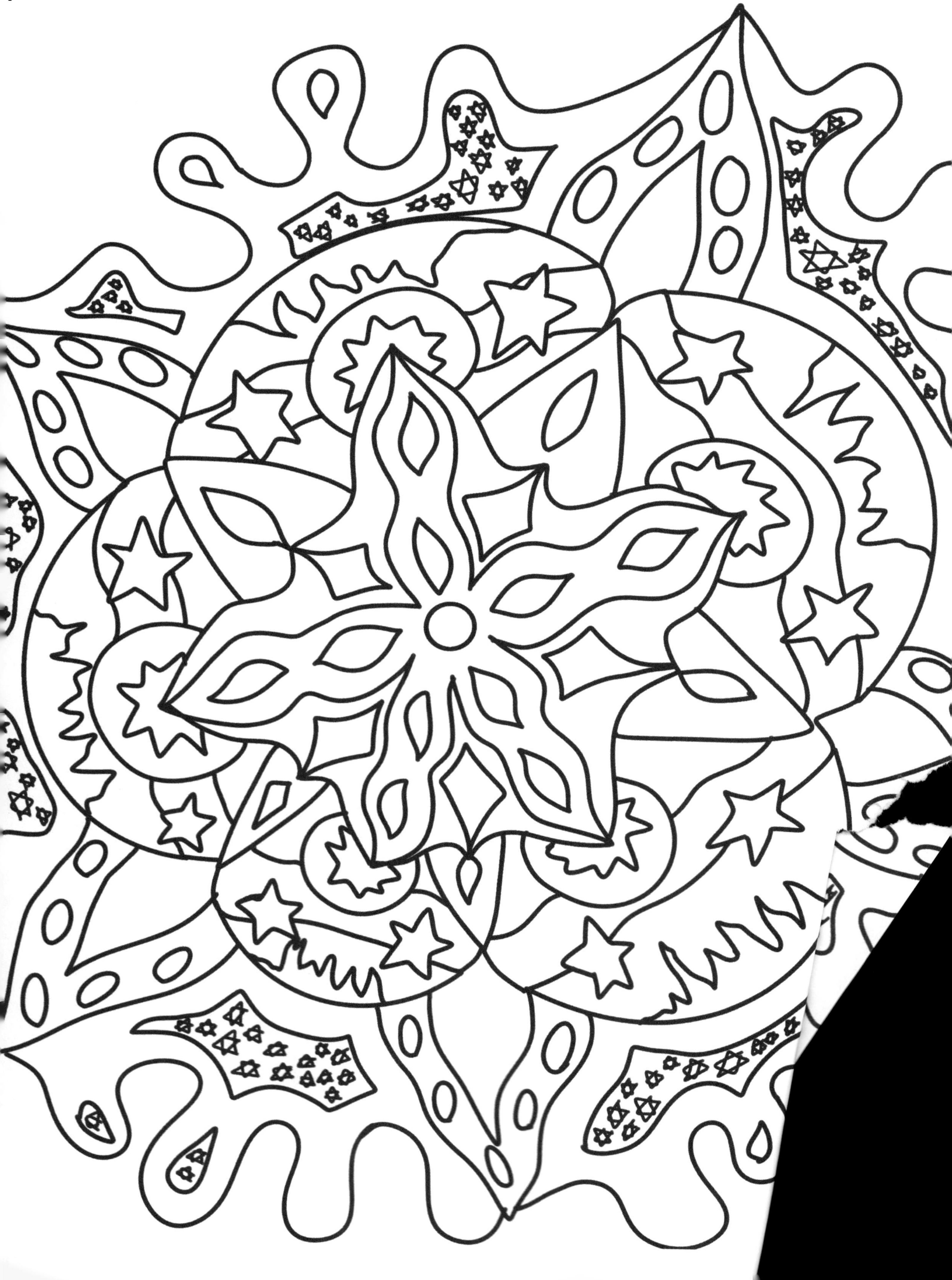

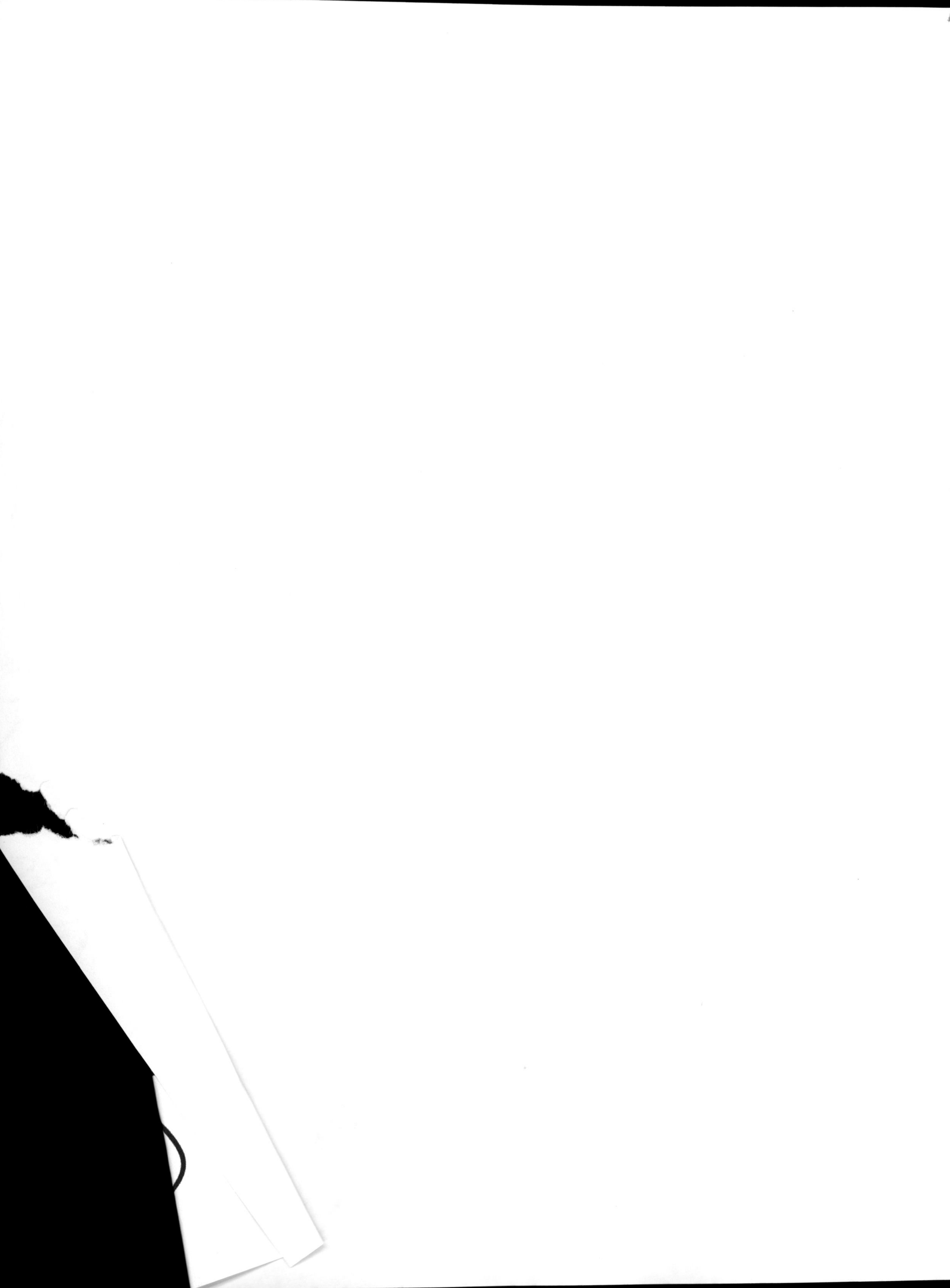

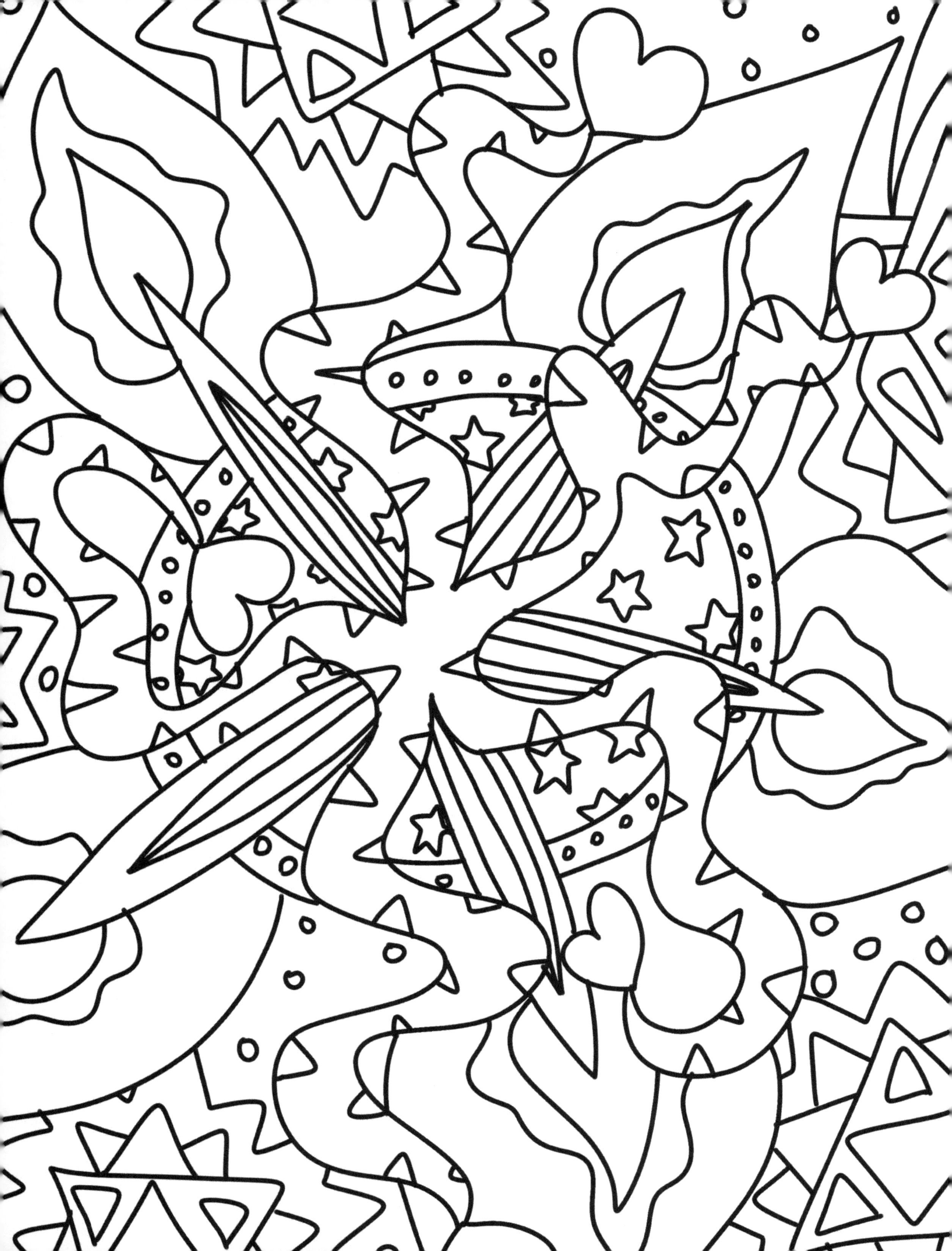

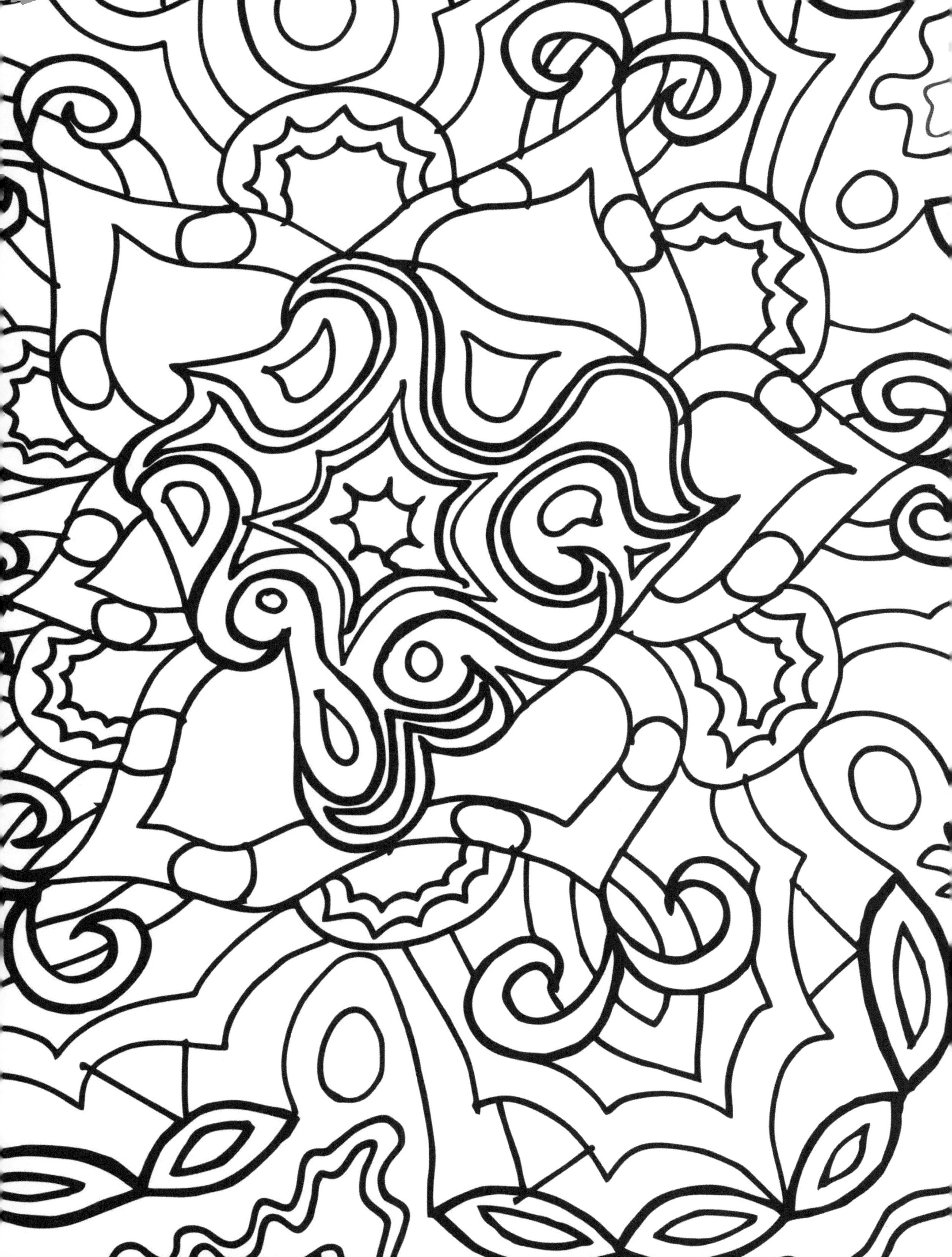

"What makes you different or weird, that's your strength."
(Meryl Streep)

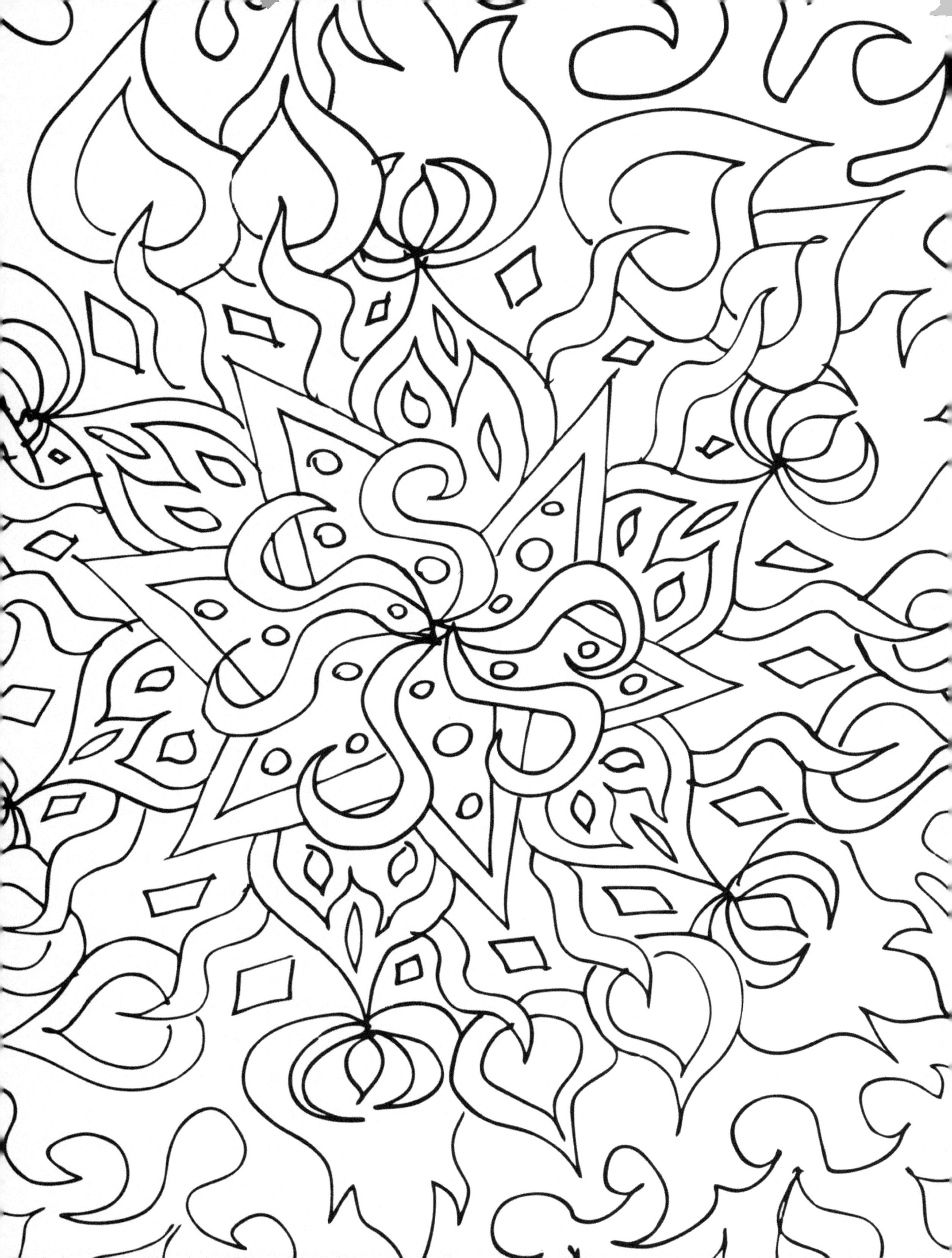

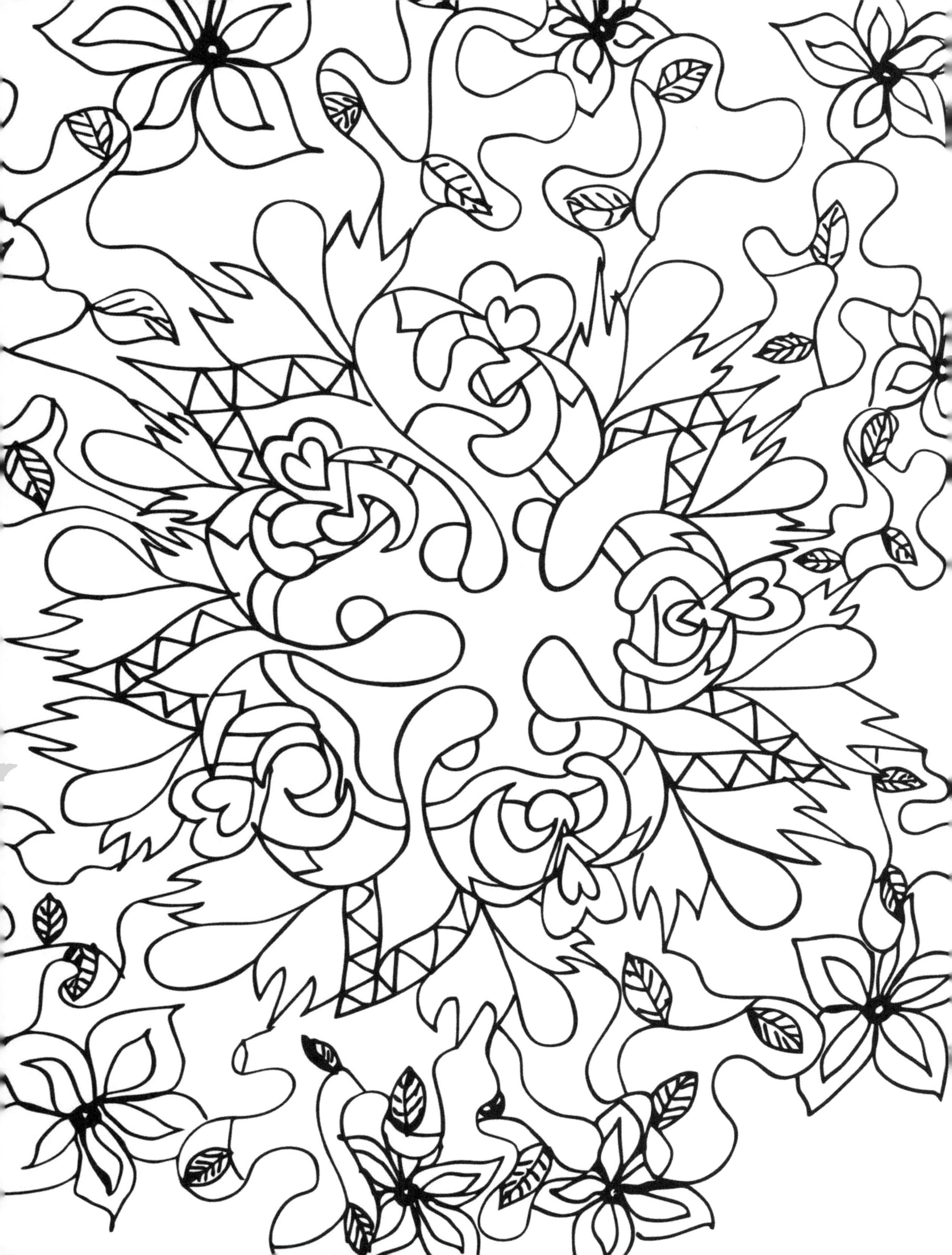

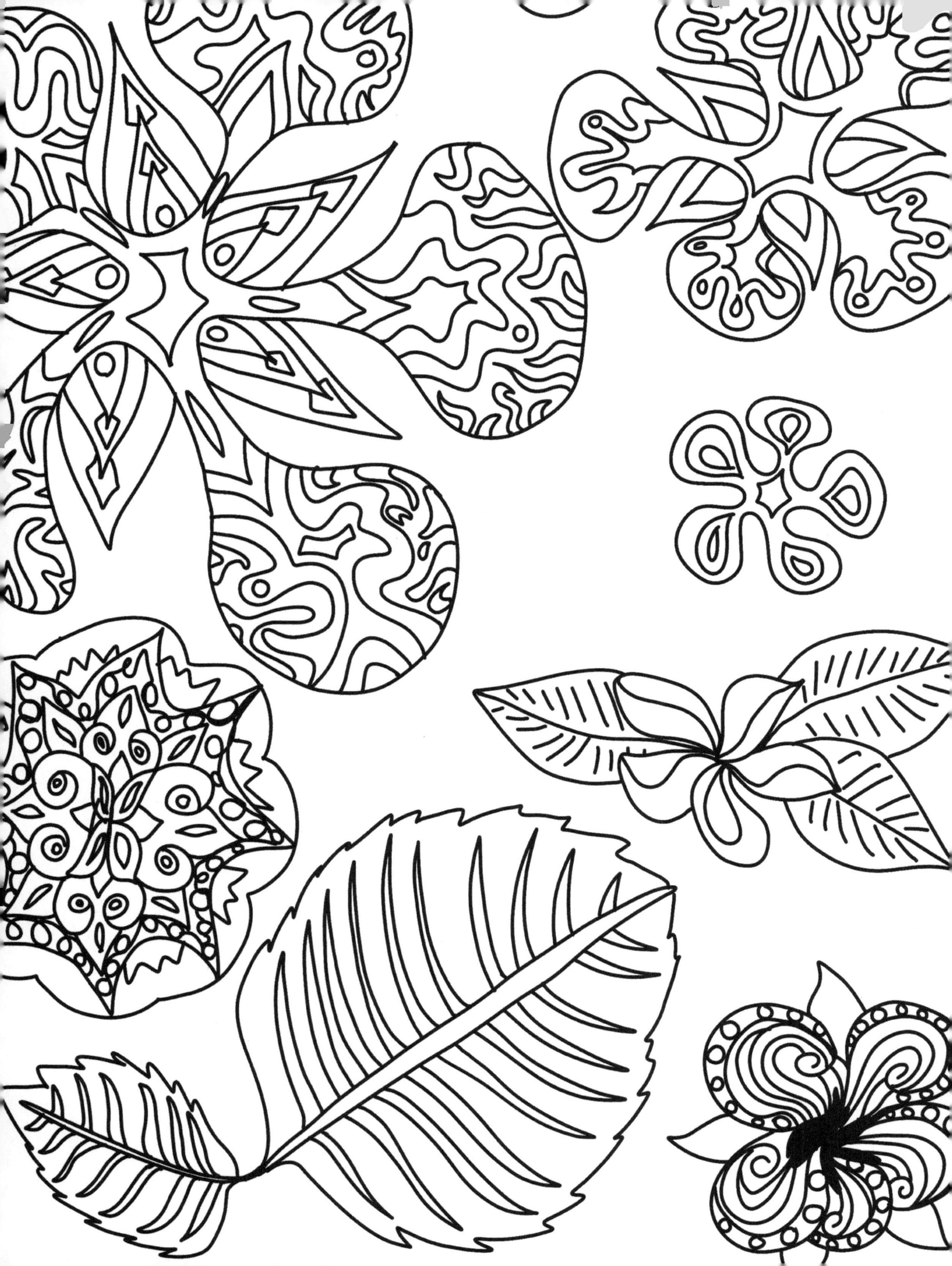

*"The only scripture you should listen to or
live by is the message of your own heart."*
(Teal Swan)

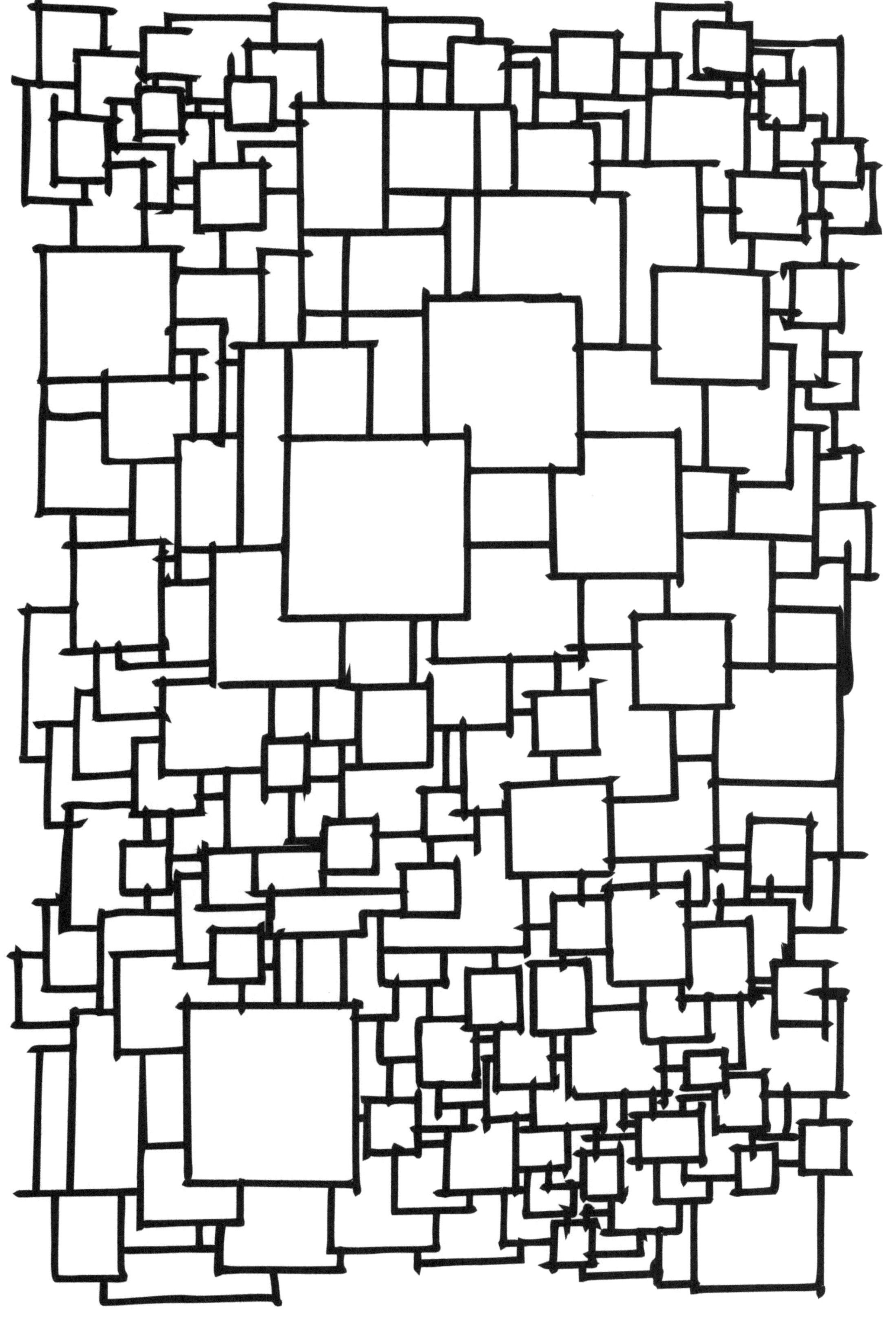

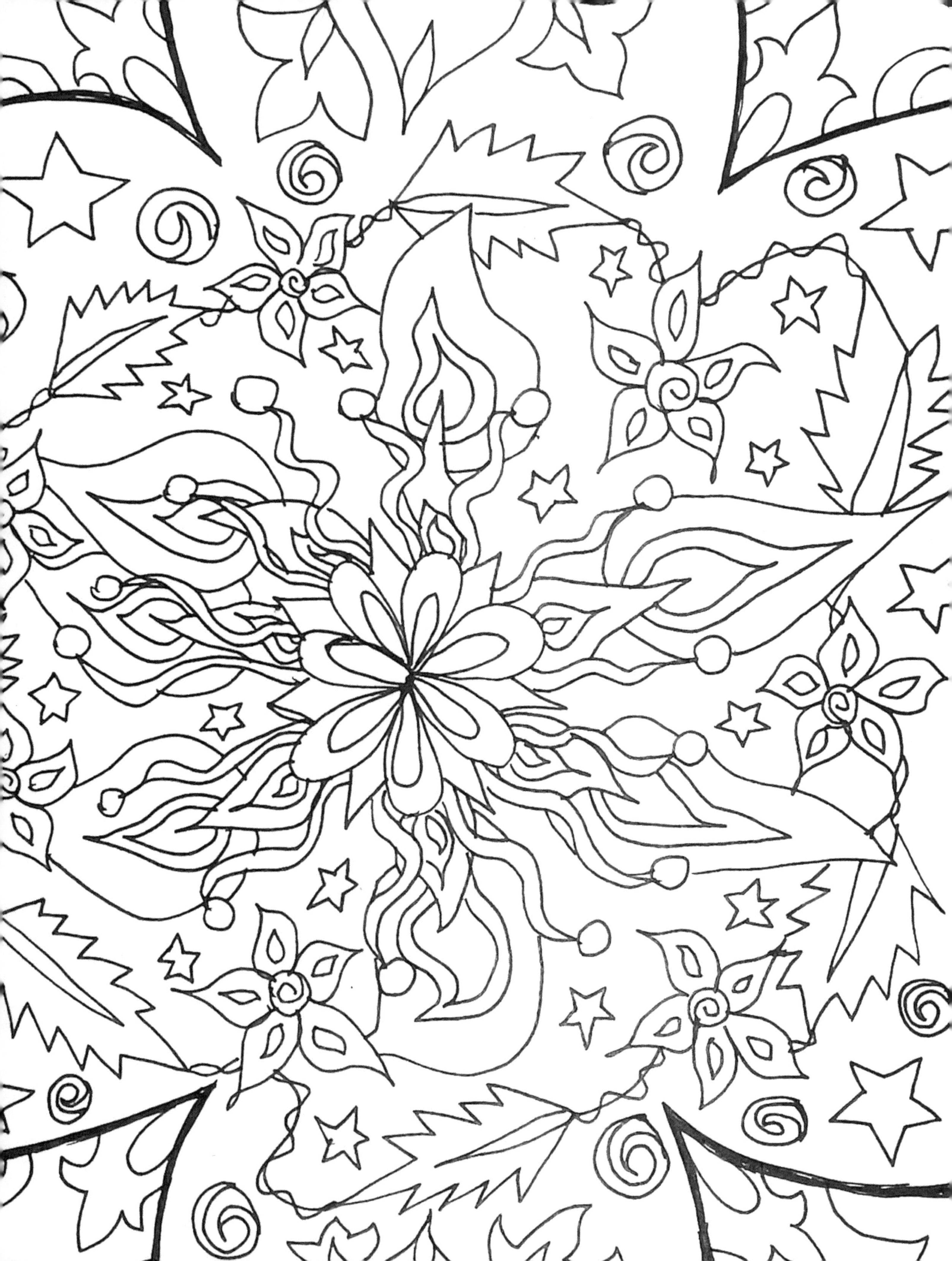

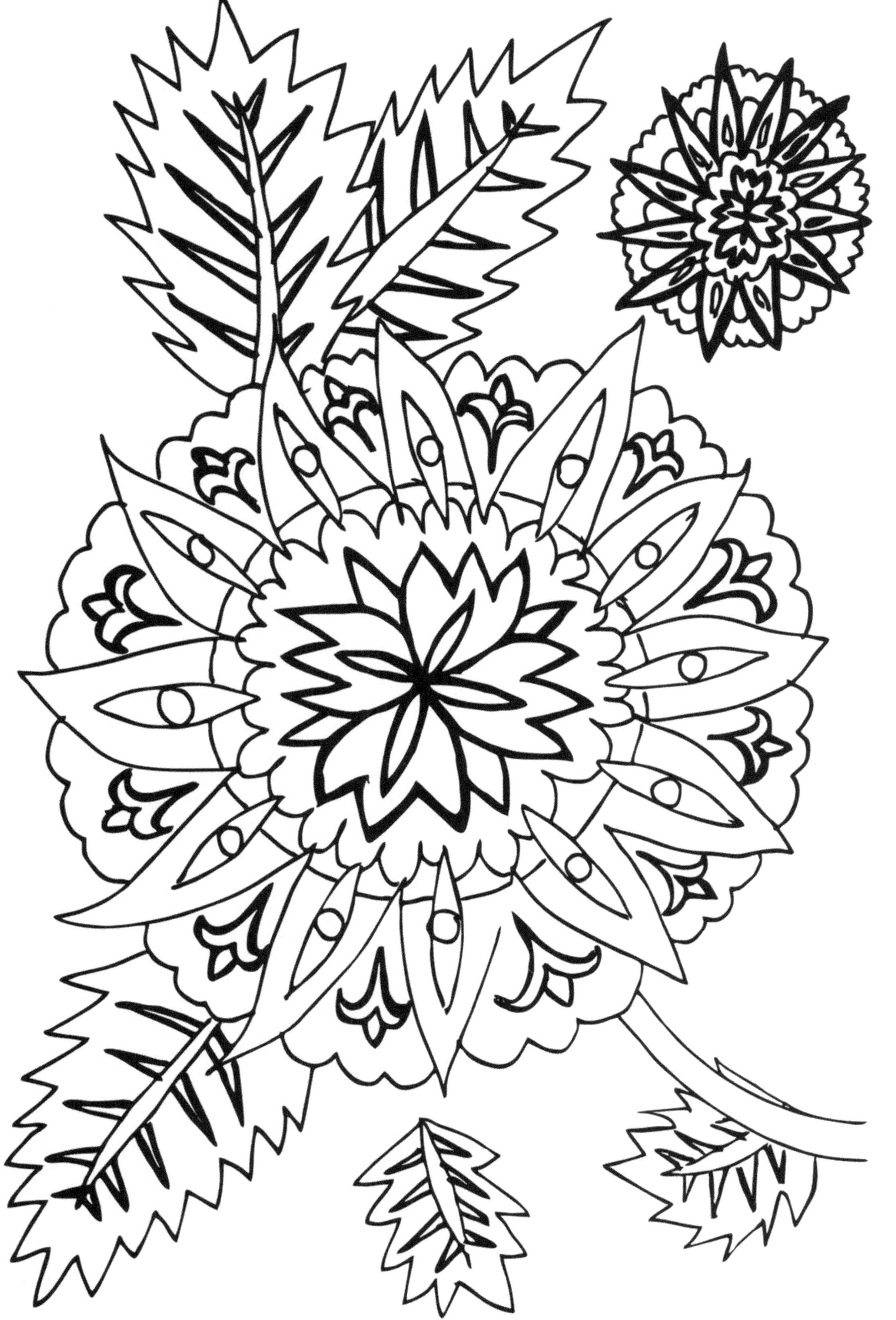

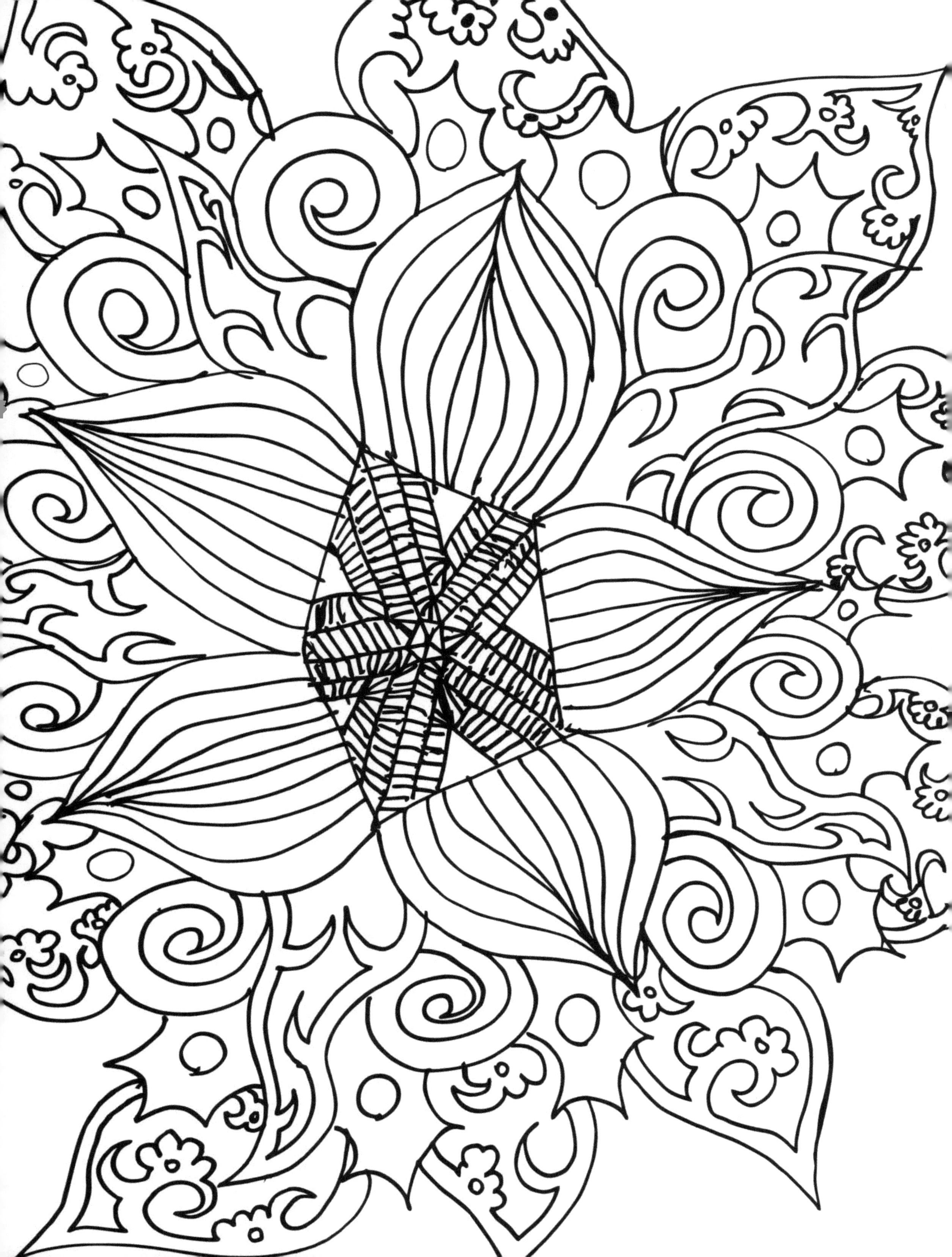

*"The meaning of life is to find your gift.
The purpose of life is to give it away."*
(Pablo Picasso)

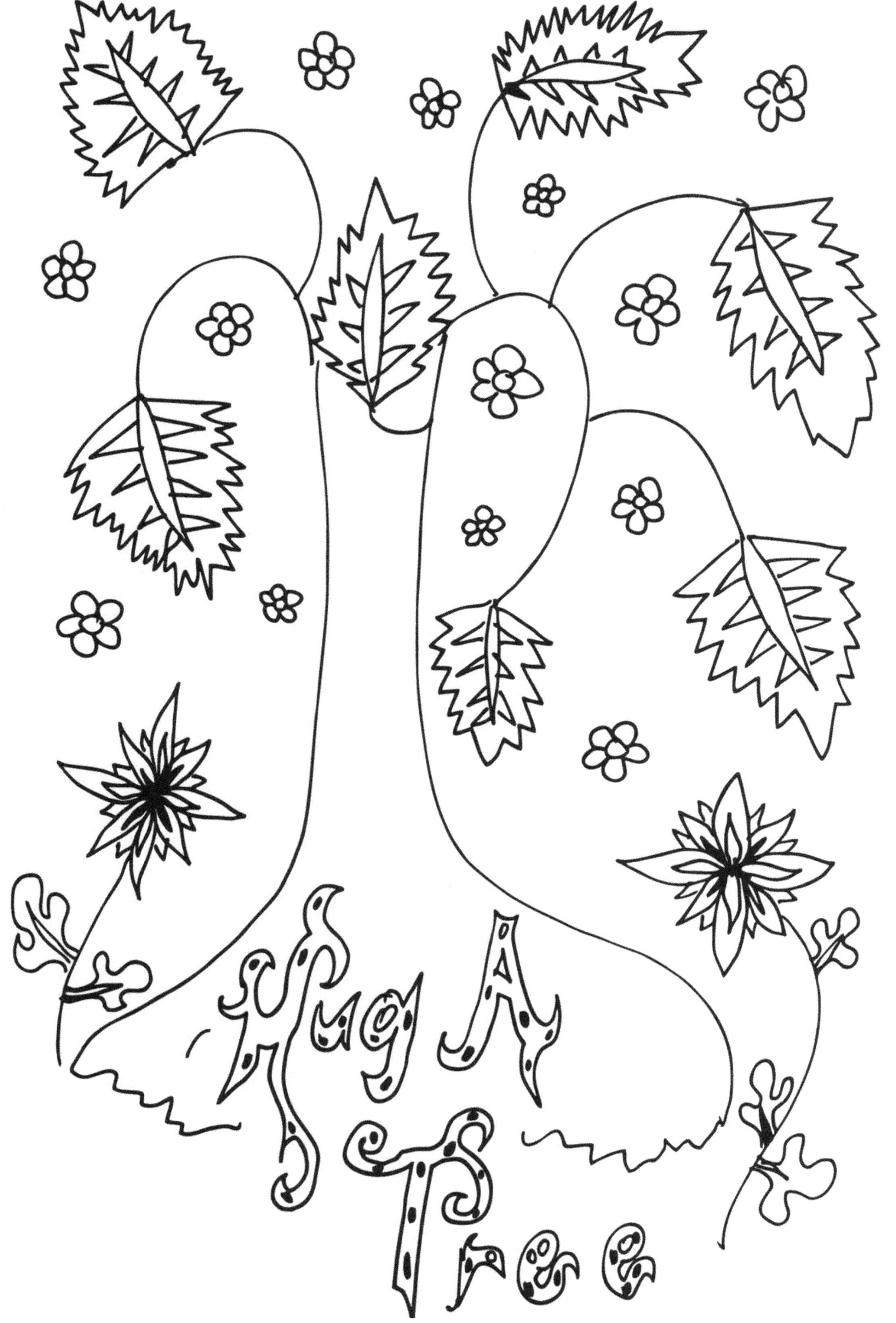
Hug A Tree

A Moment of Thanks

I want to thank all who have supported me during the creative process of my book, *Akashic Dreaming.*

To my daughter Juliette, Zak Buccanon, Dale Purchase, Aaron, my father Tony, my mother Lyn, Courtney and Kayne, Dustyn and Darcey.

To, Alison, Pam, Cathy, Ingrid, Annette, Neville, Peta, Sarah, Nicole, Nicky, Chell, Bryndal, Cade, Thomas, Micheal, Wendy and Louise.

And finally, to the team at 48 Hour Author and to the rest of my support network not mentioned, you know who you are.

Thank you to all who enjoy colouring and may you understand soul time as you express yourself throughout my book.

Tanith x

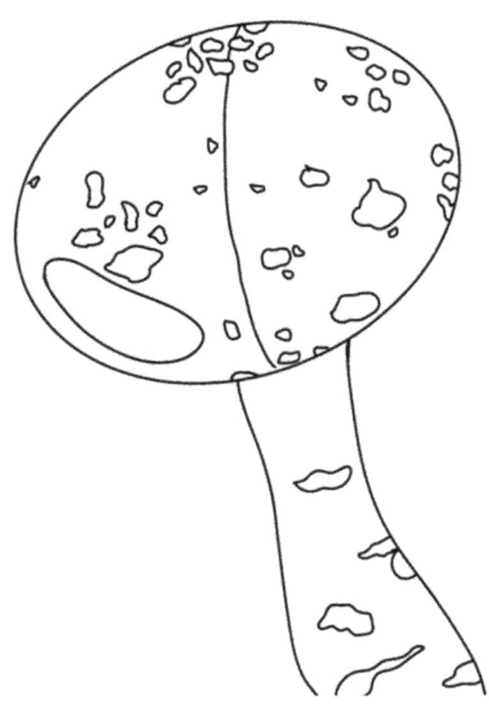

About the Author

"We are all together as students in the same classroom." (Tanith Hare)

Born artistic and developed as a creative artist, Tanith explored many outlets of creativity with different materials and textures to create works of all mediums and stature. First published in high school and pursuing a career in community service work and psychology at university, creative pursuits became a meditative and meaningful practice to relax and explore in Tanith's daily life.

Beginning her professional career after jobs in retail and hospitality and when her daughter commenced school, Tanith pursued community service work, where she assisted the youth and refugees with residential homes, domestic assistance, transportation, counselling, art therapy, and project development.

In her 30s, Tanith delved into various community service work fields, such as teacher's aide, land council education and disability support. After managing a small boarding home, Tanith observes, *"The young ones inspired and taught me about the world today through their eyes and point of view. The world is ever-changing, and today's youth need support in alternative ways compared to older generations."*